Punctuation

by Dr. Ruth Fennick

illustrated by Dianne Ellis

Publisher
Instructional Fair • TS Denison
Grand Rapids, Michigan 49544

About the Author

Dr. Ruth Fennick is co-author of three books on composition for middle school students. She has given presentations at state, national, and international conferences and has published in a variety of journals focusing on the teaching of language arts. She currently teaches writing and English/Language Arts methods courses at Illinois State University.

Instructional Fair • TS Denison grants the individual purchaser permission to reproduce the student activity materials in this book for noncommercial individual or classroom use only. Reproduction for an entire school or school system is strictly prohibited. No part of this publication may be reproduced for storage in a retrieval system, or transmitted in any form or by any means, electronic, mechanical, recording, or otherwise, without the prior written permission of the publisher. For information regarding permission, write to Instructional Fair • TS Denison, P.O. Box 1650, Grand Rapids, MI 49501.

ISBN: 1-56822-349-8
Punctuation
Copyright © 1996 by Instructional Fair • TS Denison
2400 Turner Avenue NW
Grand Rapids, Michigan 49544

All Rights Reserved • Printed in the USA

Table of Contents

End Punctuation
- Declarative and Imperative Sentences 1
- Interrogative and Exclamatory Sentences 3
- Other Uses of the Period 4

Commas
- Listening to What You Say 5
- Applying Comma Rules: Introductory Elements 6
- Compound Sentences 10
- Items in a Series 11
- Interrupters: Appositives..............................12
- Nonessential Elements 16
- Coordinating Adjectives 17
- Conventional Situations 18
- Commas in Action! 22

Semicolons
- Independent Clauses 24
- Main Clauses and Conjunctive Adverbs..............................25
- With Other Punctuation 26
- Semicolons in Action! 27

Colons
- Series and Lists 29
- Formal Quotations and Explanations..........31
- Conventional Situations 32
- Colons in Action! 33

Apostrophes
- Contractions..............34
- Possessives..............35
- Numbers, Letters, and Words..............37
- Apostrophes in Action! 38

Quotation Marks
- Direct and Indirect Quotations 39
- Unusual Expressions and Titles 43
- With Other Punctuation 44
- Quotation Marks in Action! 47

Parentheses
- Explanatory Material 48

Brackets
- Explanations Within Parentheses and Quotations 49

Dashes
- Explanation and Emphasis 50
- Appositives and Comma Series 51

Hyphens
- Compound Words and Numbers 52
- Other Uses of the Hyphen 53
- Parentheses, Brackets, Dashes, and Hyphens in Action! 54

Italics
- Titles, Names, and Words 55

Ellipsis Points
- Omissions 56

Slashes
- Lines of Poetry 57
- Italics, Ellipsis Points, and Slashes in Action! 58

Answer Key 59

About This Book

Punctuation rules often appear unnecessarily rigid and arbitrary. The activities in this book will emphasize the critical role that punctuation plays. Rather than simply following rules that create a "correct" text, writers deliberate about punctuation choices, attempting to provide readers with the best signposts for responding to the words on the page. Tradition does dictate some punctuation rules, but in many cases, marks of punctuation play key roles in conveying the writer's true meaning.

Handbooks use varying terms to describe grammatical constructions, often in an attempt to be more descriptive of their function. This book uses traditional terms (noun, verb, adjective, etc.), not because they are more accurate, but because they may be more familiar.

In the following units, each mark of punctuation begins with a general description, followed by discussion and illustration of its various uses. In many cases, sentence examples come from the work of published authors, usually from famous writers of classic fiction. These examples demonstrate that marks of punctuation are tools that writers actually use. Activities involve practice with these sentences and production of original sentences imitating the authors' models that are provided.

End Punctuation
Declarative and Imperative Sentences

 Declarative and imperative sentences end with a period. A declarative sentence simply provides information. An imperative sentence requests the reader or listener to do something.

Here are two sentences from the opening paragraph of Frances H. Burnett's book *Sara Crewe*. These are declarative sentences because they provide information.

In the first place, Miss Minchin lived in London.
On Miss Minchin's door there was a brass plate.

Here are two imperative sentences from *Sara Crewe*.

"Put your doll down," said Miss Minchin.
"Now listen to me," she went on, "and remember what I say."

Try It!
Following are six declarative sentences from the first chapter of *Sara Crewe*. Provide end punctuation where you think it is needed.

In the first place, Miss Minchin lived in London Her home was a large, dull, tall one, in a large, dull square, where all the houses were alike, and all the sparrows were alike, and where all the door knockers made the same heavy sound On Miss Minchin's door there was a brass plate On the brass plate there was inscribed in black letters *Miss Minchin's Select Seminary for Young Ladies* Little Sara Crewe never went in or out of the house without reading that door plate and reflecting upon it By the time she was 12, she had decided that all her trouble arose because, in the first place, she was not "Select," and in the second she was not a "Young Lady"

© Instructional Fair, Inc. 1 IF2723 Punctuation

Declarative and Imperative Sentences

Try It!
The next passage contains sentences from *Sara Crewe* that include both declarative and imperative sentences. Provide the necessary end punctuation, and mark each as "D" or "I" in the blank, depending on whether the sentence is declarative or imperative.

1. She had never been an obedient child ____
2. Sara kept the big odd eyes fixed on her teacher and said nothing ____
3. The truth was, Miss Minchin was in her worst mood ____
4. Don't be impudent, or you will be punished ____
5. Improve your manners ____
6. "I can speak French better than you, now," said Sara ____
7. Miss Minchin could not speak French at all and, indeed, was not in the least a clever person ____
8. You can go now ____
9. The child walked up the staircase, holding tightly to her doll ____
10. From that day her life changed entirely ____

Try It!
Think of a situation, like Sara Crewe's, when you have seen someone treated unkindly. Write two declarative sentences telling about the situation. Then write two imperative sentences telling people who find themselves in a similar situation what to do.

Declarative
  1. _____
  2. _____
Imperative
  1. _____
  2. _____

Interrogative and Exclamatory Sentences

 An interrogative sentence asks a question and is followed by a question mark.

When Sara Crewe returned to her room, she said to her doll Emily, "You are the only friend I have in the world; why don't you say something? Why don't you speak?"

 An exclamatory sentence shows strong feelings and is followed by an exclamation point.

Cold, hungry, and tired after a hard day and cruel treatment from Miss Minchin and the other girls, Sara breaks into tears and says, "I can't bear this! I know I shall die!"

Try It!
Place the appropriate punctuation (a question mark or an exclamation point) in the blank. The sample sentences come from Burnett's book *Sara Crewe*.

1. "You are nothing but a doll _____" she cried.

2. "Put your doll down _____" screamed Miss Minchin.

3. "My old shoes made me slip down in the mud, and they laughed _____"

4. "What are you staring at _____" Miss Minchin demanded sharply.

5. "Stay ____" commanded Miss Minchin, "Don't you intend to thank me____"

6. "What is the matter with you _____" Sara asked Ermengarde, who was crying over a package of books her father sent her.

7. "Don't you like reading _____" Sara asked.

8. "I hate it _____" Ermengarde replied.

© Instructional Fair, Inc. IF2723 Punctuation

Other Uses of the Period

 Use a period after initials and abbreviations.

Notice the period in each underlined abbreviation below.

> <u>Mr.</u> Crewe *(Mr. for Mister)*
> <u>Ms.</u> <u>S.</u> Crewe *(Ms. for Mistress or Miss, and S. for Sara)*
> Sara probably had to get up at 6:00 <u>A.M.</u> to do her chores.
> *(A.M. for ante meridian, which really means before noon)*
> If Sara became a doctor, she would be called <u>Dr.</u> Sara Crewe.

Try It!

1. Using your middle initial, write your name as it would appear if you became a doctor. _____

2. Using A.M. and P.M., write the times you normally get up and go to bed.

   Get up: _____

   Go to bed: _____

End Punctuation in Action!

Write a paragraph of at least five sentences telling what you think happened to Sara at Miss Minchin's Select Seminary for Young Ladies. Include in your paragraph one or more of each of the following sentence types: *declarative, imperative, interrogative,* and *exclamatory*. Identify the type of each sentence by writing the name above the sentence.

_____
_____
_____
_____
_____
_____

© Instructional Fair, Inc. IF2723 Punctuation

Commas
Listening to What You Say

How a writer punctuates a sentence affects the meaning. Look at the following sentences. How does the punctuation change the meaning?

Woman without her man is nothing.
Woman: without her, man is nothing.

Write sentences explaining the meaning of each.

1. _____

2. _____

Commas often cause writers problems because the rules sometimes seem confusing. But with a little work, you should be able to feel more confident about your use of commas. First, you need to listen to what you say when you write. Reading aloud is best, but even if you read silently, you can "hear" the rhythm and emphasis in a sentence. When we speak, we tend to pause briefly in some places and move quickly through others. We also emphasize some words and use higher or lower pitch, depending on how we want the listener to respond. When you look at punctuation marks this way, you will see that they really serve as writers' clues to their readers to read a sentence one way or another. Let's see what punctuation clues the writer of the example sentences above has given the reader.

1. Read the sentences aloud and "listen" for any pauses. Are there any words in the first sentence that cause you to pause? If so, list them. _____

2. After which word or words do you pause in the second sentence?
   _____

3. Now listen for emphasis. Look especially at the two words, *Woman* and *her.* Does the punctuation increase or decrease the emphasis? _____

Applying Comma Rules
Introductory Elements

In addition to listening for stress and pauses, you also need to memorize a few rules. Some rules reflect *conventions* rather than *meaning*, but many of them are designed to make your meaning clearer. Most of the sentence examples in this entire section are based on Sir Arthur Conan Doyle's story of "The Hound of the Baskervilles," featuring the famous detective Sherlock Holmes and his colleague Dr. Watson.

 Use a comma after introductory words, phrases, and clauses.

This comma signals your reader that the main part of the sentence comes next and often makes the meaning clearer.

> **Though Sir Charles had resided at Baskerville Hall for a short period, his friendly character had won the affection of all who came into contact with him.**

Try It!

Punctuate the following sentences to reflect the writer's probable meaning. Notice how important the comma is to the reader.

1. While Holmes and Dr. Watson were eating Dr. Mortimer appeared suddenly on their doorstep.

2. "If you clean up Dr. Mortimer and I will discuss the case," Holmes told Watson.

Try It!

Write two sentences of your own, following the patterns in the sentences above. Underline the main parts of the sentences, and put in the commas.

1. While _____
   _____
   _____

2. If _____
   _____
   _____

© Instructional Fair, Inc.   IF2723 Punctuation

Commas After Introductory Words and Phrases

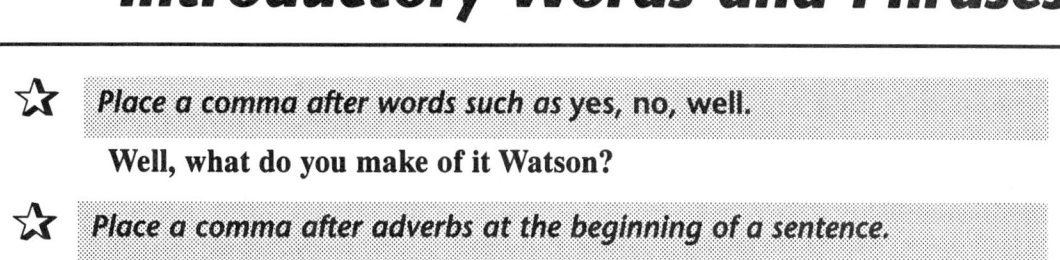

☆ *Place a comma after words such as yes, no, well.*

Well, what do you make of it Watson?

☆ *Place a comma after adverbs at the beginning of a sentence.*

Certainly, I think your deduction seems possible.

☆ *Use a comma after long introductory phrases.*

With an expression of great interest, Holmes carried the mysterious man's cane to the window and looked it over carefully.

Try It!

The following sentences require commas following introductory words or phrases. Supply the necessary commas.

1. Yes this is my friend Watson.

2. After studying the cane Holmes determined that the mysterious owner could not have been on the staff of the hospital.

3. Well how can you possibly be so sure of that?

4. Admittedly I had to put many pieces of the puzzle together to discover this.

5. In spite of your vast medical knowledge I'm afraid you are no match for me in the detective business.

Try It!

Finish the three sentences below, using the introductory words or phrases suggested. Be certain to supply commas where they are needed.

1. No _____
2. Certainly_____
3. With very little effort _____

© Instructional Fair, Inc.   IF2723 Punctuation

Commas After Introductory Clauses

 Use a comma after introductory dependent clauses (subjects and verbs that cannot stand alone as a sentence).

"Since we have been so unfortunate as to miss him, this accidental souvenir is important," said Holmes.

Try It!

The following sentences require commas after introductory clauses. Supply the necessary commas.

1. Since I had expected a typical country practitioner the appearance of our visitor was a surprise to me.

2. "If you hold these views why have you come to consult me at all?" Holmes asked Mortimer.

3. "When I caught a glimpse of something which looked like a large black calf passing at the head of the driveway he compelled me to go down to the spot where the animal had been and look around for it," Mortimer explained.

4. "If Sir Charles could have spoken with me before his death he would have warned me against bringing this last heir to that deadly place," Mortimer said.

5. "If your supernatural theory is correct it could work the young man evil in London as easily as in Devonshire," Holmes argued.

Try It!

Now try writing three sentences, each with an introductory clause, a comma, and a main clause.

1. Since_____
2. When _____
3. If _____

Commas in Review: After Introductory Words, Phrases, and Clauses

Try It!

The following sentences require commas after introductory words, phrases, or clauses. Provide the necessary commas.

1. If we take this as a working hypothesis we have a fresh basis from which to start our identification of this unknown visitor.

2. Obviously when Dr. Mortimer withdrew from the service of the hospital to start practice for himself, the cane was given to him by his friends.

3. As he entered his eyes fell upon the stick in Holmes's hand.

4. Yes it is a statement of a certain legend which runs in the Baskerville family.

5. In spite of his considerable wealth he was simple in his personal tastes.

6. Had the findings of the coroner not finally put an end to the romantic stories which have been whispered in connection with the affair it might have been difficult to find a tenant for Baskerville Hall.

Try It!

Using the introductory words provided below, write original sentences. Supply the necessary commas following the introductory word, phrase, or clause.

1. Curiously _____

2. With _____

3. When _____

Commas in Compound Sentences

 Use commas in compound sentences (two or more independent clauses joined by coordinating conjunctions and, but, or, for, yet).

Holmes was sitting with his back to me, and I had given him no sign of my occupation.

 Do not use a comma before the conjunction if what follows is not a complete sentence.

Holmes was sitting with his back to me and had no sign of my occupation.

Try It!

All but one of the following sentences require commas to separate the independent clauses. Supply the necessary punctuation.

1. The day had been wet and Sir Charles's footmarks were easily traced down the alley.

2. He then proceeded down the alley and discovered the body at the far end.

3. No signs of violence were discovered upon Sir Charles's person but the doctor's evidence pointed to an almost incredible facial distortion.

4. Dr. Mortimer refused at first to believe that it was his friend and patient who lay before him but he knew such symptoms were possible in cases of death from cardiac exhaustion.

5. Holmes was silent but his little darting glances showed me the interest which he took in our curious companion.

Try It!

Write one compound sentence predicting what you think may have happened to Sir Charles Baskerville. Be certain that you have complete sentences on both sides of the comma and the conjunction.

Commas Between Items in a Series

 Use a comma between words, phrases, or clauses in a series.

Words: It was a dignified, solid, and reassuring stick that the old-fashioned family practitioner used to carry.

Phrases: Holmes leaned back, put his fingertips together, and assumed his most impassive and judicial expression.

Clauses: Dr. Mortimer withheld information from the coroner because he felt that a man of science should not indorse popular superstition, that Baskerville Hall would remain untenanted, and that no practical good would result from confiding his suspicions.

Try It!

Use commas to separate each series of words, phrases, or clauses.

1. Sir Charles's illness his interest in science and his love of travel caused us to spend many pleasant hours together.

2. One evening three weeks before the fatal event, I drove up to Sir Charles's house descended from my gig and stood in front of him.

3. Suddenly, I saw his eyes fix themselves over my shoulder with an expression of disbelief fear and horror.

4. On the night of his death, Sir Charles declared his intention of starting out the next day for London ordered Barrymore to prepare his luggage and went out as usual for his nocturnal walk.

5. At twelve o'clock Barrymore, finding the hall door still open, became alarmed lighted a lantern and went in search of his master.

Try It!

Write a sentence describing three possible causes of Baskerville's death. Separate your causes by commas.

_____

_____

© Instructional Fair, Inc.　　　　　IF2723 Punctuation

Commas with Interrupters: Appositives

 Use commas with interrupters—words or expressions that interrupt the flow of a sentence.

 Use commas to set off an appositive (a noun or pronoun following another noun or pronoun that identifies or explains it). The appositive can come in the middle of the sentence or at the end.

What does Dr. James Mortimer, the man of science, ask of Sherlock Homes, the specialist in crime?

 If the appositive is a proper name, no comma is used.

The butler Barrymore made the discovery of Sir Charles Baskerville's body.

Try It!
Use commas to set off the appositives in the following sentences.

1. Dr. James Mortimer the friend and medical attendant of the deceased has given evidence as to Sir Charles's failing health.

2. Mr. Stapleton a mutual friend who was much concerned at his state of health was of the same opinion.

3. The youngest brother Rodger Baskerville was the only other kinsman we have been able to trace.

4. This is evidently a case of extraordinary interest one which presented the scientific expert with immense opportunities.

5. And you a trained man of science believe it to be supernatural?

Try It!
Choose two sentences from the activity above to imitate, using your own words to create new sentences. For example, sentence 1 could be rewritten, "Stephen King, the popular writer of scary stories, has also written scripts for movies."

_____

_____

Commas with Interrupters
Parenthetical Expressions

 Use commas to set off parenthetical expressions used to explain or qualify a statement. Some common expressions include **indeed, I hope, for example, of course, too.**

The murder was, indeed, a mystery.

"This stick, though originally a very handsome one, has been so knocked about that I can hardly imagine a town practitioner carrying it," said Dr. Watson.

Try It!
Use commas to set off the parenthetical expressions in the following sentences.

1. Sir Charles's ancestor Hugo Baskerville according to the legend of the Hound of the Baskervilles was attacked by a huge black beast, shaped like a hound, yet larger than any hound that ever a mortal eye has rested upon.

2. Baskerville's companions seeing the beast turn its blazing eyes and dripping jaws upon them shrieked with fear.

3. One it is said died that very night of what he had seen.

4. Many of the family it cannot be denied have been unhappy in their deaths, which have been sudden, bloody, and mysterious.

5. Charles was the very image they tell me of the family picture of old Hugo Baskerville.

Try It!
Write two sentences using the parenthetical expressions provided. Set off the parenthetical expressions with commas before and after.

1. _____ you must admit _____

_____

2. _____ for example _____

_____

© Instructional Fair, Inc. 13 IF2723 Punctuation

Commas with Interrupters
Direct Address and Direct Quotations

 Use commas to set off a noun in direct address whether it comes at the beginning, middle, or end of a sentence.

Watson, what do you make of it?
I make nothing of it, my dear Watson, nothing at all.

 Use commas to set off direct quotations.

"Perfectly sound," said Holmes.
"I think," said I, "that Dr. Mortimer is a successful, elderly medical man."

Try It!

Use commas to set off the direct quotations and direct address in the following sentences. Some sentences require several commas.

1. "Such is the tale my sons of the coming of the hound, which is said to have plagued the family so sorely ever since" Baskerville's letter said.

2. "Since the tragedy Mr. Holmes there have come to my ears several incidents which are hard to reconcile with the settled order of Nature" Mortimer explained.

3. "Put into plain words" said Holmes "there is a diabolical agency which makes Dartmoor an unsafe abode for a Baskerville—is that your opinion?"

4. "At least I might go the length of saying that there is some evidence that this may be so" Mortimer responded.

5. Now Mr. Holmes what would you advise me to do?

Try It!

Write two sentences, one as Sherlock Holmes and one as Dr. Mortimer. Include both dialogue and direct address, using commas correctly.

_____

_____

Review: Commas with Interrupters

Try It!

Each of the sentences below contains an interrupter that should be set off by commas. Insert commas where they are needed.

1. "I must thank you" said Sherlock Holmes "for calling my attention to a case which certainly presents some features of interest."

2. I came to you Mr. Holmes because I recognized that I am myself an unpractical man with a most serious and extraordinary problem.

3. The legend of the Hound of the Baskervilles a story of great suffering and tragedy was passed on by my Baskerville ancestors.

4. Sir Charles as is well known made large sums of money in South African speculations.

5. "His heart was affected" Dr. Mortimer explained "and the constant anxiety in which he lived was evidently having a serious effect upon his health."

6. Incredible as it may appear to you Mr. Holmes he was honestly convinced that a dreadful fate overhung his family.

7. It is understood that the next of kin is Mr. Henry Baskerville the son of Sir Charles Baskerville's younger brother.

8. Your advice as I understand it is that the young man will be as safe in Devonshire as in London?

9. The young man when last heard of was in America.

10. "Oh Dr. Mortimer to think that you may not have called me in!" exclaimed Sherlock Holmes.

© Instructional Fair, Inc.   IF2723 Punctuation

Commas with Nonessential Elements

 Use commas to set off nonessential word groups describing nouns or pronouns. A word group is considered nonessential if the meaning of the sentence would not change greatly without it.

Mr. Sherlock Holmes, who was usually very late in the mornings, was seated at the breakfast table.

On the desk lay the letter, which bore a most peculiar inscription.

Try It!

Each of the sentences below contains a nonessential element that should be set off by commas. Insert the necessary commas.

1. This family paper was committed to my care by Sir Charles Baskerville whose sudden and tragic death some three months ago created so much excitement in Devonshire.

2. I had the story from my father who also had it from his father.

3. The recent death of Sir Charles Baskerville whose name has been mentioned as a probable candidate in the next election has cast a gloom over the country.

4. The doctor's explanation of Sir Charles's condition was borne out by the post-mortem examination which showed long-standing organic disease.

5. It was important that the case be settled so that heirs could carry on for Sir Charles whose good work had been so sadly interrupted by his death.

Try It!

Sometimes it is difficult to tell whether a word group is essential or nonessential. Read the sentence below to see how commas affect meaning.

The second Baskerville brother who died young is the father of this lad Henry.
The second Baskerville brother, who died young, is the father of this lad Henry.

1. Without commas, how many brothers probably died young? _____

2. With commas, how many brothers probably died young? _____

Commas with Coordinating Adjectives

 Use a comma between coordinating adjectives.

The visitor's walking cane was a fine, thick piece of wood.

Try It!

Each of the sentences below contains coordinating adjectives that should be set off by commas. Insert the necessary commas.

1. "I have, at least, a well-polished silver-plated coffee pot in front of me," Holmes said.

2. Dr. Mortimer is a successful elderly doctor.

3. He was a tall thin man with a long nose like a beak, which jutted out between keen gray eyes.

4. He had long quivering fingers as agile and restless as the antennae of an insect.

5. Dr. Mortimer turned the manuscript to the light and read in a high cracking voice the following curious old-world narrative.

Try It!

Draw two objects, then write sentences describing them. Use coordinating adjectives separated by commas.

Objects   **Sentences**

1. _____
   _____
   _____

2. _____
   _____
   _____

Commas in Conventional Situations

 Use commas to set off items in dates and addresses.

The account of Sir Charles Baskerville's mysterious death was reported in the Devon County *Chronicle* of May 14, 1884.

Dr. James Mortimer
Charing Cross Hospital
London, England

 Use commas after the salutation of a friendly letter and after the closing in formal and informal letters.

Dear Sherlock,

Sincerely,

Try It!

If Sherlock Holmes had sent the following letter to his friend Watson, how would he have punctuated it? Insert commas where necessary.

November 27 1885

Dear Watson

Dr. James Mortimer published two articles about unusual human behavior. "Some Freaks of Atavism" was published in the journal *Lancet* dated April 11 1882. "Do We Progress?" was published in the *Journal of Psychology* on March 30 1883.

These articles could be useful in solving this case. Please arrange to have copies sent to me at Baskerville Hall in Devon England.

Sincerely

Sherlock

Commas in Review
Introductory Elements, Compound Sentences, Items in a Series, Interrupters, Nonessential Elements, Coordinating Adjectives

Try It!

Each of the sentences below omits required commas. Provide the necessary commas. Some sentences require the addition of more than one comma.

1. These are the public facts Mr. Holmes in connection with the death of Sir Charles Baskerville.

2. Although he would walk in his own grounds nothing would induce him to go out upon the moor at night.

3. The idea of some ghastly presence constantly haunted him and more than once he asked me whether I had ever seen any strange creature or heard the baying of a hound on my medical journeys at night.

4. Before the terrible event occurred several people had seen a creature which corresponds with this Baskerville demon and could not possibly be any animal known to science.

5. They all agreed that it was a huge creature—luminous ghastly and spectral.

6. Sir Charles lay on his face his arms out his fingers dug into the ground and his features convulsed with some strong emotion.

7. Although Barrymore did not see any marks upon the ground around the body Dr. Mortimer reported that he observed fresh clear footprints.

8. Dr. Mortimer who looked strangely at us for an instant spoke almost in a whisper as he answered "Mr. Holmes they were the footprints of a gigantic hound!"

Commas in Review
Conventional Uses

Try It!

Pretend that Sherlock sent the following letter to Watson. How would he have punctuated it? Supply the necessary commas.

September 16 1886

Dear Sherlock

Enclosed are the copies you requested. I agree that the Baskerville case sounds quite intriguing.

Further information about the history of the Baskerville family can be obtained at the British Library Russell Street London.

Sincerely

Watson

Try It!

Now write your own letter to Sherlock Holmes asking about the case on which he is working. Tell him that you have read about the mysterious death of Sir Charles Baskerville and would like more information about it. Tell him where to write to you to send the information. Be certain to include all necessary commas.

Review: Multiple Comma Rules

Try It!

Each of the following sentences omits commas reflecting multiple comma rules. See whether you can supply all the missing commas. (The number in parentheses following each sentence tells you how many commas are needed.)

1. Holmes leaned forward in his excitement and his eyes had the hard dry glitter which shot from them when he was keenly interested. (2)

2. Of course if Dr. Mortimer's surmise should be correct and we are dealing with forces outside the ordinary laws of Nature there is an end of our investigation. (3)

3. I could not call you in Mr. Holmes without disclosing these facts to the world and I have already given my reasons for not wishing to do so. (3)

4. At ten o'clock tomorrow Dr. Mortimer I will be much obliged to you if you will call upon me here and it will be of help to me in my plans for the future if you will bring Sir Henry Baskerville with you. (3)

5. I recommend sir that you take a cab call off your spaniel who is scratching at my front door and proceed to Waterloo to meet Sir Henry Baskerville. (5)

6. Our clients were punctual to their appointment for the clock had just struck ten when Dr. Mortimer followed by the young baronet was shown up. (3)

7. The latter was a small alert dark-eyed man about thirty years of age very sturdily built with thick black eyebrows and a strong pugnacious face. (5)

8. "Now" said Sir Henry Baskerville "perhaps you will tell me Mr. Holmes what in thunder is the meaning of this and who it is that takes so much interest in my affairs?" (5)

9. "Really Mr. Holmes this exceeds anything which I could have imagined" said Dr. Mortimer gazing at my friend in amazement. (4)

© Instructional Fair, Inc. IF2723 Punctuation

Commas in Action!

Try It!

Think of some mystery story, like "The Hound of the Baskervilles," that you recall from childhood or from more recent reading or movies. If you prefer, think up an original story of your own. Write your story here. Do not worry yet about getting all of the commas right. You can do that when you revise. Give your story a title.

Correcting Comma Use in Revision

Try It!

Writers usually do not think much about punctuation as they are writing, but later, when they are polishing their writing, they pay close attention to it. Now that you have finished writing your story, you, too, need to take a closer look at your punctuation.

To gain practice in the various uses of the comma, see whether you can revise your story to include sentences using each of the seven rules. Look back to review each rule. Then place check marks in the blanks below to indicate which rules you have used. (Do not forget to read your story out loud to see whether you can hear the pauses and the emphasis.)

____ Introductory Elements   ____ Nonessential Elements

____ Compound Sentences   ____ Coordinating Adjectives

____ Elements in a Series   ____ Conventional Uses

____ Interrupters

Semicolons with Independent Clauses

A semicolon signals the end of a thought and represents a pause longer than that of a comma but not as complete as a period. As with end punctuation and commas, your voice drops and you naturally pause at the place where the semicolon is needed. The sentences in this section are based on the book *Black Beauty* by Anna Sewell, who used semicolons frequently in her writing. The story is told in first person from the point of view of the horse.

 Use a semicolon to connect main clauses without a coordinating conjunction.

There were six young colts in the meadow besides me; they were older than I was.

 Do not use a semicolon if the main clauses are joined by a coordinating conjunction (and, or, nor, for, but). Instead, use a comma before the conjunction.

Sometimes we had rather rough play, for they would bite and kick, as well as gallop.

Try It!

Most of the sentences below contain main clauses that need to be separated by semicolons. Read them aloud; then supply the necessary semicolons. If a sentence requires a comma instead, supply the comma.

1. One day when there was a good deal of kicking, my mother whinnied to me to come to her she said, "I want you to pay attention to what I am going to say."

2. "You have been well bred and well born your father has a great name in these parts, and your grandfather won the cup at the races."

3. I have never forgotten my mother's advice I knew she was a wise old horse, and our master thought a great deal of her.

4. My mother loved our master very much and she would neigh with joy and trot up to him when she saw him at the gate.

Semicolons with Main Clauses and Conjunctive Adverbs

 Use a semicolon between independent clauses joined by connecting words such as however, for example, that is, in fact. *These words are usually followed by commas.*

Black Beauty's mother took good care of her colt; in fact, she kept him close by her side day and night.

Try It!
Rewrite the following sentences to create one sentence using a connecting word or phrase like *however*, *for example*, *that is*, or *in fact*. Use a semicolon before the connecting word and a comma following it.

1. Dick, a hired boy on the farm, often teased the horses. He sometimes threw stones at them.

   _____
   _____

2. When Black Beauty's master found out about Dick's treatment of the horses, he was very angry. He was so mad that he fired Dick and told him never to come back.

   _____
   _____

Try It!
In the example sentence below, the two main clauses are joined by the connecting words *for example*. Try writing the main clauses two other ways: (1) as two separate sentences, and (2) as one sentence connected by a semicolon without the connecting words *for example*.

Black Beauty's mother taught him proper horse etiquette; for example, she told him that he should never kick or bite.

1. _____
   _____

2. _____
   _____

Semicolons with Other Punctuation

 Usually commas are used to separate items in a series, but when the items themselves contain commas, the reader can get confused. Semicolons make these sentences clearer and easier to read.

When Black Beauty was four years old, Squire Gordon set out to break him, which meant teaching him to wear a saddle and bridle; to carry on his back a man, woman, or child wherever they wanted to go; and to do it quietly.

 Similarly, although commas normally separate main clauses joined by coordinating conjunctions (and, or, nor, but, for), when the main clauses contain commas, semicolons can make the meaning clearer.

Besides this, the horse has to learn to wear a collar and a breeching, to stand still while they are put on, to have a cart or a buggy fixed behind, so that he cannot walk or trot without dragging it after him; and he must go fast or slow, just as his driver wishes.

Try It!
The sentences below contain commas that could be confusing. Replace commas with semicolons to make the sentence easier to read. Cross out the comma and write in a semicolon above the sentence.

1. Our master gave us good food, good lodging, and kind words, and he spoke as kindly to us as he did to his little children.

2. The horse must never start at what he sees, nor speak to other horses, nor bite, nor kick, nor have any will of his own, but always do his master's will, but the worst of all is that, when his harness is once on, he may neither jump for joy nor lie down for weariness.

Try It!
Using one of the sentences above as a model, write your own original sentence, imitating the form and the punctuation.

_____

_____

Semicolons in Action!

The following passage from *Black Beauty* contains numerous sentences using semicolons. In this section Black Beauty describes the difficulty of learning to wear a saddle, horseshoes, and a harness. Read the passage aloud, listening for the pauses where the author has placed semicolons.

> After the bit and bridle came the saddle; my master put it on my back very gently, while Old Daniel held my head. He then made the girths fast under my body, patting and talking to me all the time; then I had a few oats, then a little leading about, and this he did every day till I began to look for the oats and the saddle. The next business was putting on the iron shoes; that was very hard at first. The blacksmith took my feet in his hand, one after the other, and cut away some of the hoof. Then he took a piece of iron the shape of my foot and clapped it on and drove some nails through, so that the shoe was firmly on. And now having got so far, my master went on to break me to harness; there were more new things to wear. First, a stiff heavy collar just on my neck, and a bridle with great side-pieces against my eyes, called blinders; and blinders they were, for I could not see on either side but only straight in front of me. Next there was a small saddle with a strap that went right under my tail; that was the crupper. I hated the crupper—to have my long tail doubled up and poked through that strap was almost as bad as the bit. I never felt more like kicking, but of course I could not kick such a good master, so in time I got used to everything and could do my work as well as my mother.

Different writers have different writing styles. Some use shorter sentences, with little need for semicolons, while others use longer sentences. As you can see, the author of *Black Beauty*, Anna Sewell, uses semicolons frequently in her writing.

1. Count the total number of sentences in the above paragraph. _____

2. Now count the number of sentences containing semicolons. _____

3. Rewrite one of the semicolon sentences, making two short sentences.

   _____

   _____

4. Which do you prefer? Why? _____

   _____

Using Semicolons in Original Writing

Try It!

Imitate Anna Sewell's writing style by writing a story using numerous semicolons. Like Sewell, you may want to write as though you were a horse, dog, or other pet, and tell of the treatment that you got from your master. After writing your paragraph, underline the sentences containing semicolons. Read your story aloud (and check the rules) to be certain that you have used the semicolons correctly.

Colons
with Series and Lists

Colons are used to call the reader's attention to what is coming. Some writers use colons frequently, whereas others rarely use them. One writer who used them often is Willa Cather, whose sample sentences in this section come from her book *O Pioneers!* This story tells of the people who settled the Nebraska prairie.

 Use a colon after a main clause to direct the reader's attention to a list. In the following sentences Cather describes the wildflowers on the Nebraska prairie and the interests of some of the young immigrants.

> **The wild flowers disappeared, and only in the bottom of the gullies grew a few of the very toughest and hardiest: shoestring, ironweed, and snow-on-the-mountain.**
>
> **The French boys like a bit of swagger, and they were always delighted to hear about anything new: new clothes, new games, new songs, new dances.**

Try It!
Following are two sentences, each followed by a colon. Supply a list to complete the sentence.

1. I like many different kinds of food, but I have several favorites: _____

2. My friends and I like to play different types of games, but some of them we play over and over: _____

Try It!
Now follow the same pattern to write a sentence completely on your own, using a colon followed by a list.

_____

_____

Misuse of the Colon with Series and Lists

 Do not use a colon immediately following a verb. The colon must be preceded by a full independent clause.

    Incorrect: Cather's stories tell about the difficulties of immigrants who were: Russian, Swedish, Bohemian, French, and other nationalities.

Try It!
Correct the sample sentence by writing it without the colon. There should be no punctuation between *were* and *Russian*.

_____

 Do not use a colon immediately following a preposition.

    Incorrect: Cather's book tells of: the joys, accomplishments, hardships, and tragedies of pioneer life.

Try It!
Correct the sample sentence by rewriting it without the colon.

_____

 Do not use a colon after these words: such as, especially, including.

    Incorrect: Another famous Cather book, *My Antonia*, tells about entertainment in Nebraska in the 1800s, such as: attending plays, going to dances, and celebrating holidays.

Try It!
Correct the sample sentence by rewriting it without the colon.

Colons with Formal Quotations and Explanations

 Use a colon to introduce formal quotations.

He closed the book and repeated these words softly: "He sendeth the springs into the valleys, which run among the hills; they give drink to every beast of the field."

Try It!
Write two sentences introducing formal quotations. The first sentence has been started for you. Don't forget to use quotation marks.

1. One of my favorite songs begins with these lyrics: " _____
   _____."
2. _____
   _____

 Use a colon to introduce a statement of explanation (a second sentence that explains, summarizes, or restates the first).

Isn't it strange: there are only two or three human stories, and they go on repeating themselves as fiercely as if they had never happened before.

At last he seemed to see a ray of hope: his sister was coming, and he got up and ran toward her in his heavy shoes.

Try It!
Write two sentences imitating the two sample sentences above. The first one has been started for you.

1. Isn't it strange: _____
   _____
2. _____
   _____

Colons in Conventional Situations

 Use a colon to separate hours and minutes when writing time.

10:55 A.M.

 Use a colon after the salutation in a formal letter.

Dear Ms. Johnston:

Try It!
Fill in the blanks using colons correctly.

1. Look at the clock. What time is it right now? _____
2. Write a formal salutation to your teacher. _____

Review: Colons

Try It!
The following sentences require colons to introduce a series, to introduce a statement of explanation, to introduce a quotation, and to indicate the time. Supply the necessary colons.

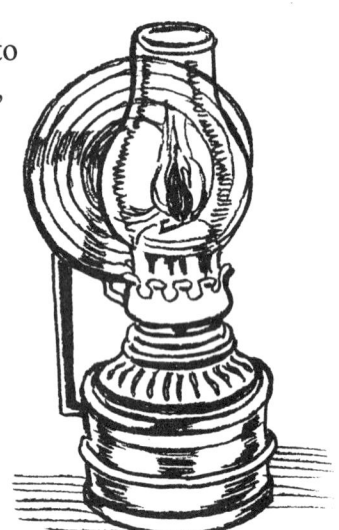

1. He disliked the litter around human dwellings the bits of broken china, the broken food, the old wash-boilers and tea-kettles thrown into the sunflower patch.

2. The light fell upon the two sad young faces that were turned mutely toward it upon the eyes of the girl, who seemed to be looking with perplexity into the future, and upon the eyes of the boy, who seemed already to be looking into the past.

3. In a moment she heard Emil and Raoul singing these words
   "Across the Rio Grand-e
   There lies a sunny land-e
   My bright-eyed Mexico!"

4. People in pioneer days had difficulty reading after 9 00 P.M. because they had no electricity, and candles or coal lamps offered little light.

© Instructional Fair, Inc.   IF2723 Punctuation

Colons in Action!

Try It!
Write a short, formal letter to your favorite movie or TV star. Include in your letter sentences using colons to introduce a series, to introduce a quotation, and to explain a statement. Mention a particular time in your letter, using the colon correctly. Remember to use a colon following the salutation. Include all the necessary parts of a letter, as indicated by the lines and directions in brackets.

_____ (date)

_____ (person's name)
_____ (street address)
_____ (city/state/zip code)

_____ (salutation)

_____
_____
_____
_____
_____
_____
_____

_____ (closing)

_____ (signature)

Apostrophes with Contractions

The apostrophe is used to show ownership or possession, to signal the omission of a letter or letters in a word, and to form plurals of letters, numbers, and words.

> ☆ *Use an apostrophe when letters have been omitted in a contraction. A contraction is created when two words are combined to make one word, leaving out some letters. The apostrophe signals to the reader the omission of letters.*

Two Words	Contraction	Letter(s) Omitted
it is	it's	i
he has	he's	ha
she would	she'd	woul

Try It!
What letters have been omitted in the following contractions?

Two Words	Contraction	Letter(s) Omitted
1. I will	I'll	_____
2. you are	you're	_____
3. could have	could've	_____

Try It!
Write the two words for these contractions, and identify the omitted letter(s).

Two Words	Contraction	Letter(s) Omitted
1. _____	he's	_____
2. _____	let's	_____

Try It!
Write the contractions for these words, and identify the omitted letter(s).

Two Words	Contraction	Letter(s) Omitted
1. I have	_____	_____
2. It is	_____	_____

Apostrophes with Possessives Singular and Plural Nouns

Apostrophes show ownership or possession of something.

☆ *For singular nouns, use an apostrophe and -s to form the possessive case.*

        Jane's bike   **a week's pay**

☆ *For plural nouns that do not end in -s, use an apostrophe and -s.*

        children's games   **women's names**

☆ *For plural nouns that end in -s, add only the apostrophe.*

        books' covers   **dogs' collars**

Try It!
Below are two columns, one for the singular possessive form and one for the plural possessive form. Fill in the blanks with the appropriate possessive form.

	Singular Possessive	**Plural Possessive**
1.	woman's car	_____
2.	_____	bicycles' tires
3.	pencil's eraser	_____
4.	_____	doctors' orders

☆ *Use an apostrophe and -s to form the possessive case of indefinite pronouns.*

        somebody's   **nobody's**   **anyone's**

☆ *Do not use apostrophes with the possessive forms of personal pronouns (its, hers, his, ours, yours, theirs).*

        The wagon train lost <u>its</u> wheel in the river.

Try It!
Write two sentences, one using an indefinite pronoun from the list above and one using a possessive form of one of the personal pronouns.

1. _____
2. _____

Apostrophes with Possessives Compound Words

★ *To form the possessives of compound words (words made up of two or more words, often hyphenated), add an apostrophe and -s to the last part of the compound or hyphenated word.*

        anyone else's   **sister-in-law's**

★ *To show joint ownership, add an apostrophe and -s to the last name.*

        Andrea and Emmanuel's house

★ *To show separate ownership, add an apostrophe and -s to each name.*

        Andrea's and Emmanuel's bikes

Try It!
In the passage below, the apostrophes have been omitted. Write the correct form of the word or words on the line at the right.

1. My brother-in-laws car is red. _____
2. Saras and Sams glasses were broken in the soccer game. _____
3. Have you seen Jonathan and Erins baby brother? _____
4. Someones books were left in the cafeteria. _____
5. I thought they were Nora's, but they were somebody elses. _____

Try It!
Now write one sentence of your own illustrating each of the rules above.

1. Possessive compound word: _____

_____

2. Joint ownership: _____

_____

3. Separate ownership: _____

_____

Apostrophes with Numbers, Letters, Words

> ⭐ *Use an apostrophe to show the plurals of letters, numbers, and words referred to as words. Years can be written with an apostrophe or without.*

I earned all A's in that class.
Ice skaters like to do figure 8's.
Try to limit your *And's* at the beginning of sentences.
1990s or 1990's

Try It!
Provide the information requested using apostrophes to show plurals of letters, numbers, words, and years.

1. If I study hard, I will earn all _____ (grades of B).

2. My math teacher says she cannot read my _____ and _____ (numbers 5 and 8).

3. The baby sitter told my little sister that she did not want to hear any more _____ (the word no).

4. I love to read about the men and women who settled the frontier in the _____ (the last century).

Apostrophes in Review

Stephen Crane, in *The Red Badge of Courage*, used many contractions. Use the information in brackets to write the words as Crane wrote them.

1. A river, amber-tinted in the shadow of [belonging to *it*] _____ banks, purled at the [belonging to the *army*] _____ feet.

2. "[What is] _____ up, Jim?'

3. He could not put faith in [belonging to *veterans*] _____ tales.

4. "I think [they will] _____ fight better than some, if worse than others."

5. "[That is] _____ the way I figure."

6. "Well," he said profoundly, "[I have] _____ thought it might get too hot for Jim Conklin."

Apostrophes in Action!

Try It!
Following is a passage from Stephen Crane's *The Red Badge of Courage* in which the young hero tells his mother that he has joined the army, a decision he later regrets. The passage contains seven words that need apostrophes. Circle the words, supply the apostrophes, and write the words correctly in the blanks.

"Ma, Im going to enlist."

"Henry, dont you be a fool," his mother had replied. She had then covered her face with the quilt. There was an end to the matter for that night. Nevertheless, the next morning he had gone to a town that was near his mothers farm and had enlisted in a company that was forming there. When he had returned home his mother was milking the brindle cow.

"Ma, Ive enlisted," he had said to her diffidently. There was a short silence.

"The Lords will be done, Henry," she had finally replied, and had then continued to milk the brindle cow. When he had stood in the doorway with his soldiers clothes on his back, he had seen two tears leaving their trails on his mothers scarred cheeks.

1. _____ 2. _____ 3. _____ 4. _____
5. _____ 6. _____ 7. _____

Try It!
Write a paragraph of your own telling of a time when you did something that you later regretted. In your paragraph, use at least seven words that require apostrophes, and circle them. Use words in the list above if they fit your story.

Quotation Marks
Direct and Indirect Quotations

Quotation marks are used to enclose the exact words of a speaker. Many of the sentences in this section are based on Louisa May Alcott's book *Little Women*.

☆ *Place quotation marks before and after a direct quotation.*

"Christmas won't be Christmas without any presents," grumbled Jo, lying on the rug.

☆ *If the name of the speaker interrupts the quotation, place quotation marks before and after the words spoken. Notice that the second part of the quotation begins with a lowercase letter if it is a continuation of the first part.*

"I don't believe any of you suffer as I do," cried Amy, "for you don't have to go to school with impertinent girls, who plague you if you don't know your lessons, and laugh at your dresses."

☆ *Do not use quotation marks with indirect quotations, which tell what someone said but do not use their exact words.*

Amy said she didn't think her sisters understood her problem.

Try It!

Supply the necessary quotation marks in the following sentences. Some sentences may not need quotation marks.

1. I'll tell you what we'll do said Beth, we'll each get Mother something for Christmas and not get anything for ourselves.

2. Meg told her sisters that they could surprise their mother with the gifts.

3. Meg said, I shall give her a nice pair of gloves.

4. Some handkerchiefs, all hemmed said Beth.

5. I'll get a little bottle of cologne. She likes it, and it won't cost much, so I'll have some left to buy my pencils, added Amy.

Quotations with Long Passages

☆ *When quoting long passages (about four lines or more), set off the passage by indenting ten spaces from the left margin. Because the indented lines signal the reader that this is quoted material, quotation marks are not used.*

In the following passage from *Little Women*, Alcott describes Jo, one of the main characters of the novel:

> Fifteen-year-old Jo was very tall, thin, and brown, and reminded one of a colt, for she never seemed to know what to do with her long limbs, which were very much in her way. She had a decided mouth, a comical nose, and sharp, gray eyes, which appeared to see everything, and were by turns fierce, funny, or thoughtful.

Try It!

Write an introduction (like the one above) for a story that you like. Then copy four or more lines, indenting the passage and omitting quotation marks. The introduction has been started for you.

In the following passage from _____ [title of story]

_____
_____
_____
_____

_____
_____
_____
_____
_____
_____
_____
_____
_____

Quotations with Dialogue

> ☆ *When writing dialogue, signal speaker changes by starting a new paragraph. In the following passage from Alcott's* Little Women, *the two sisters Amy and Jo argue about appropriate language and conduct.*

"Jo does use such slang words!" observed Amy with a reproving look at the long figure stretched on the rug.

Jo immediately sat up, put her hands in her pockets, and began to whistle.

"Don't Jo. It's so boyish!"

"That's why I do it."

"I detest rude, unladylike girls!"

"I hate affected, niminy-piminy girls!"

Try It!

Supply the necessary quotation marks in the following passage.

On New Year's Eve, Meg was preparing to go to a special party and asked Jo to curl her hair with the hot tongs.

Ought they to smoke like that? asked Beth from her perch on the bed.

It's the dampness drying, replied Jo.

What a strange smell! It's like burned feathers, observed Amy, smoothing her own pretty curls with a superior air.

There, now I'll take off the papers and you'll see a cloud of little ringlets, said Jo, putting down the tongs.

Try It!

In the next passage, the dialogue has been improperly run together. Supply the necessary quotation marks, and underline each word that should be indented to begin a new paragraph (to indicate the words of each new speaker).

Oh, oh, oh! What have you done? I'm spoiled! I can't go! My hair, oh, my hair! wailed Meg, looking with despair at the frizzle on her forehead. You shouldn't have asked me to do it. I'm sorry, but the tongs were too hot, groaned poor Jo. It isn't spoiled. Just frizzle it, and tie your ribbon so the ends come on your forehead, and it will look like the latest fashion, said Amy consolingly. I wish I'd let my hair alone, cried Meg. So do I. It was so smooth and pretty. But it will grow out again, said Beth.

Quotations Within Quotations

> ★ *Use single quotation marks for a quotation within a quotation. If the quotation within the quotation continues to the end of the sentence, use both single and double quotation marks after the last word.*

"The parts of my story that were taken straight out of real life are denounced by critics as impossible and absurd, and the scenes that I made up out of my own silly head are pronounced 'charmingly natural, tender, and true.'"

Try It!
Following is a passage from Louisa May Alcott's *Little Women*, in which one of the characters is telling a story. The double quotation marks have been supplied. Add the necessary single quotation marks.

The narrator began, "Once upon a time, there were four girls, who had enough to eat and drink and wear, a good many comforts and pleasures, and kind friends and parents who loved them dearly, and yet they were not contented. These girls were anxious to be good and made many excellent resolutions, but they did not keep them very well, and were constantly saying, If only we had this, or If we could only do that, quite forgetting how much they already had and how many things they actually could do. So they asked an old woman what spell they could use to make them happy, and she said, When you feel discontented, think over your blessings and be grateful."

Try It!
Write a very short story using quotations within quotations. Use single and double quotation marks where needed. The story has been started for you.

The narrator began, "Once upon a time _____
_____
_____
_____
_____
_____

Quotations with Unusual Expressions and Titles

★ *Enclose a word in quotation marks to show it being used in a special way.*

Beth's father called her "Little Miss Tranquillity," and the name suited her, for she seemed to live in a happy world of her own.

As the word "brotherly" passed through his mind in one of his reveries, he smiled and glanced up at the picture of Mozart that was before him.

Try It!
Write two sentences of your own imitating the examples above, one using a nickname and one using a word as a word. Put quotation marks around the words used in a special way.

1. _____
   _____
2. _____
   _____

★ *Enclose titles of songs, poems, short stories, articles, chapters in books, and TV episodes within quotation marks. (For titles of longer works, such as books or magazines, use italics or underlining rather than quotation marks.) Do not put quotation marks around your own titles.*

"Clementine"   "The Road Not Taken"   "The Tell-Tale Heart"

Try It!
Write the title of your favorite song, poem, and story in the blanks provided. Also, write the title of something you have written yourself.

Song Title: _____
Poem Title: _____
Story Title: _____
Original Title: _____

Quotations with Other Punctuation

☆ *Periods and commas go inside quotation marks.*

The four young faces on which the firelight shone brightened at Beth's cheerful words but darkened again as Jo said sadly, "We haven't got Father, and shall not have him for a long time."

She didn't say "perhaps never," but each silently added it, thinking of Father far away, where the fighting was.

☆ *The colon and semicolon usually go outside the quotation marks.*

"Louisa May Alcott's novel brings to life vividly the life of New England during the nineteenth century": life there was tranquil, secure, and productive.

Alcott's biographers point out that *Little Women* draws on "the rich details of her own and her family's experiences"; the story tells of her life in Concord, where she lived with her parents and three sisters.

Try It!

Supply quotation marks for the words and phrases in bold type, putting them appropriately before or after the other punctuation in the sentence.

1. Because the four sisters in *Little Women* admired Charles Dickens's *The Pickwick Papers*, they started a writers' club, which they called **The Pickwick Club**.

2. The girls created pen names to protect their identity in **The Pickwick Club**: Meg called herself **Samuel Pickwick**; Jo took the name **Augustus Snodgrass**; Beth called herself **Tracy Tupman**; and Amy became **Nathaniel Winkle**.

3. Their poems and stories appeared in a newspaper they called *The Pickwick Portfolio*, which published local news, funny advertisements, original tales, and poetry with such unusual titles as **The History of Squash**, a story about a vegetable, and **A Lament for S. B. Pat Paw**, a poem about a runaway cat.

Quotations with Other Punctuation

> ⭐ *Question marks and exclamation points go inside the quotation marks if they are part of the quotation. If not, they go outside.*

Inside Quotation Marks

"It's so dreadful to be poor!" sighed Meg, looking down at her old dress.

"Don't you wish we had the money Papa lost when we were little, Jo?" asked Meg.

Outside Quotation Marks

According to biographers, "Alcott published her first full length book at the age of twenty-two"!

Did you know that, according to biographers, Alcott used money from the sales of her books to make life "more comfortable and less of a daily struggle for her parents"?

Try It!
Following are five sentences. In the blank, write "C" if they are punctuated correctly. If they are incorrect, make changes in the sentences.

_____ 1. "Just a year ago we were groaning over the dismal Christmas we expected to have. Do you remember?" asked Jo.

_____ 2. "Rather a pleasant year on the whole!" said Meg, smiling.

_____ 3. "I'm glad it's over, because we've got you back"! said Beth, who sat on her father's knee.

_____ 4. "Rather a rough road for you to travel, my little pilgrims. But you have got on bravely!" exclaimed Mr. March, looking with affection at the girls.

_____ 5. "How do you know? Did Mother tell you" asked Jo?

Quotation Marks in Review

Try It!

The following sentences from Alcott's *Little Women* have the quotation marks removed. Supply quotation marks where needed. Be careful to put other punctuation where it belongs (before or after the quotation marks). This passage deals with Jo's sadness after the death of her sister Beth and the family's encouragement of Jo's writing.

1. Why don't you write? That always used to make you happy, said Jo's mother.

2. I've no heart to write, and if I had, nobody cares for my things, Jo replied.

3. We do. Write something for us, and never mind the rest of the world, her mother encouraged. Try it, dear. I'm sure it would do you good and please us very much.

4. I don't believe I can, Jo said. But she got out her desk and began to overhaul her half-finished manuscripts.

5. Her father told her that her story was good and he sent it, much against her will, to one of the popular magazines where newspapers copied it, and strangers as well as friends admired it.

6. I don't understand it. What can there be in a simple little story like that to make people praise it so? Jo asked, quite bewildered.

7. There is truth in it, Jo, that's the secret. You wrote with no thoughts of fame and money and put your heart into it, her father said.

8. If there is anything good or true in what I write, it isn't mine; I owe it all to you and Mother and Beth, said Jo.

9. Letters from many people told her that something in her story went straight to the hearts of those who read it.

10. So, taught by love and sorrow, Jo continued to write her little stories, thanking her readers for kindly welcoming what she called her humble wanderers.

© Instructional Fair, Inc.   IF2723 Punctuation

Quotation Marks in Action!

Try It!

Interview several family members or classmates about their favorite songs, poems, or short stories. Ask them what they like and why they like them. Take notes from these interviews and write a short essay about their responses. Try to use direct quotations, titles, definitions, and special emphasis words.

If you prefer, write a short essay about one of your own favorite poems, songs, or short stories. Copy words and sentences exactly as they appear in written form, using quotation marks correctly. Try to use direct quotations, titles, definitions, and special emphasis words. Give your paragraph a title (but remember that you do not use quotation marks for your own titles).

Parentheses
Explanatory Materials

> ☆ *Parentheses are used to set off explanatory material or material that is so loosely related to the main thought that it could be placed in a separate sentence or dropped altogether. The examples in this section are from Lewis Carroll's* Alice's Adventures in Wonderland.

So she was considering, in her own mind (as well as she could, for the hot day made her feel very sleepy and stupid), whether the pleasure of making a daisy-chain would be worth the trouble of getting up and picking the daisies when suddenly a White Rabbit with pink eyes ran close by her.

Try It!
Each of the following sentences from *Alice's Adventures in Wonderland* contains passages that Lewis Carroll placed in parentheses. Find these passages and enclose them in parentheses.

1. Alice did not think it so very much out of the way to hear the Rabbit say to itself, "Oh dear! Oh dear! I shall be late!" when she thought it over afterwards, it occurred to her that she ought to have wondered at this.

2. After falling down the hole, Alice exclaimed, "Why, I wouldn't say anything about it even if I fell off the top of the house!" which was very likely true.

3. Alice said, "I wonder what Latitude or Longitude I've got to?" she had no idea what Latitude was, or Longitude either, but thought they were nice grand words to say.

4. "Curiouser and curiouser!" cried Alice she was so much surprised that for the moment she quite forgot how to speak good English.

Try It!
Imitate the following sentence from *Alice's Adventures in Wonderland* by filling in the blanks to make a sentence of your own using parentheses.

Alice said, "Dinah'll miss me very much tonight!" (Dinah was the cat).

_____ said, "_____"
(_____).

Brackets: Explanations Within Parentheses and Quotations

★ *Use brackets to set off material within parentheses.*

Alice's Adventures in Wonderland has been a favorite ever since its publication over a century ago (it was first printed in 1865 [Macmillan], but because of printing errors, it was reprinted a year later by a second New York publisher [Appleton]).

★ *Use brackets to add material to a quotation.*

As Alice was falling and falling down the rabbit hole, she feared that she would never stop: "I must be getting somewhere near the centre [British spelling for *center*] of the earth," she said to herself.

Try It!
Supply brackets in the appropriate places in the following sentences.

1. Alice tried to guess how far the center of the earth would be: "Let me see that would be four thousand miles down, she loved talking about what she'd learned even if no one was there to listen—yes, that's about the right distance."

2. "I wonder if I shall fall right through the earth! How funny it'll seem to come out among the people that walk with their heads downward! obviously, she needed some geography lessons."

Try It!
The following sentence includes parentheses within Alice's statement. Insert a comment of your own into the parentheses by placing brackets around your suggestion for the name of a possible country.

She tried to remember the name of the country that she would find on the other side of the earth: "The Antipathies, I think—(she was rather glad there was no one listening this time, as it didn't sound at all the right word [she probably meant _____ _____])—but I shall have to ask them what the name of the country is, you know."

Dashes with Explanation and Emphasis

☆ *Use a dash to introduce explanatory material or to make something stand out for strong effect. These sample sentences come from Booker T. Washington's autobiography* Up from Slavery.

"The earliest impressions I can now recall are of the plantation and the slave quarters—the latter being the part of the plantation where the slaves had their cabins."

"In the days of slavery not very much attention was given to family history and family records—that is, black family records."

Try It!
The sentences below require dashes. In the blanks provided, write the word before the dash and the word following the dash.

1. "There was a door to the cabin that is, something that was called a door but the uncertain hinges by which it was hung, and the large cracks in it, to say nothing of the fact that it was too small, made the room very uncomfortable."

   _____ — _____

2. "In addition to these openings there was, in the lower right-hand corner of the room the 'cat-hole' a contrivance which almost every mansion or cabin in Virginia possessed during the antebellum period."

   _____ — _____

3. "The most distinct thing that I now recall in connection with the scene was that some man who seemed to be a stranger (A United States officer, I presume) made a little speech and then read a rather long paper the Emancipation Proclamation, I think."

   _____ — _____

Dashes with Appositives and Comma Series

> ⭐ *Use dashes to set off appositives (words that rename nearby nouns) or lists containing commas.*

"Three children—John, my older brother, Amanda, my sister, and myself—had a pallet on the dirt floor, or, to be more correct, we slept in and on a bundle of filthy rags laid upon the dirt floor."

Try It!
Booker T. Washington used dashes in the following sentences to set off appositives. Supply the dashes where you think Washington put them.

1. "Finally we reached our destination a little town called Maiden, which is about five miles from Charleston, the present capital of the state."

2. "I have not spoken of that which made the greatest and most lasting impression on me, and that was a great man the noblest, rarest human being that it has ever been my privilege to meet. I refer to the late General Samuel Armstrong."

Dashes in Review

Try It!
The following sentences from *Up from Slavery* include dashes for emphasis, appositives, and explanatory material. Insert the necessary dashes.

1. "I had learned from somebody that the way to begin to read was to learn the alphabet, so I tried in all the ways I could think of to learn it all of course without a teacher, for I could find no one to teach me."

2. "As yet no free schools had been started for coloured people in that section, hence each family agreed to pay a certain amount per month, with the understanding that the teacher was to "board 'round" that is, spend a day with each family."

3. "Most of the students were men and women some as old as forty years of age."

4. "I felt that a new kind of existence had now begun that life would now have a new meaning."

Hyphens with Compound Words and Numbers

☆ *Use a hyphen between two or more words which form a compound (one word made of two or more words). When several words act as an adjective in front of a noun, use hyphens between them. The following sentence from Jack London's story "To Build a Fire" illustrates both uses of the hyphen.*

Day had broken cold and gray, exceedingly cold and gray, when the man turned aside from the main Yukon trail and climbed the high earth-bank, where a dim and little-travelled trail led eastward through the fat spruce timberland.

☆ *Use a hyphen to write out numbers from twenty-one to ninety-nine.*

It was seventy-five below zero.

Try It!
Follow the instructions below for each use of the hyphen.

1. The following sentence uses a hyphen to create a compound word. Insert the hyphen and write the hyphenated word in the blank.

    It was all pure white, rolling in gentle undulations where the ice jams of the freeze up had formed. _____

2. The following sentence uses a hyphen to connect adjectives that modify a noun. Insert the hyphen and write the hyphenated word in the first blank. In the second blank, write the noun that is described by the hyphenated adjectives.

    North and south, as far as his eye could see, it was unbroken white, save for a dark hairline that curved and twisted from around the spruce covered island to the south.

    _____   _____

3. The following sentence uses a hyphen to separate words in a number. Insert the hyphen and write the hyphenated number in the blank.

    Since the freezing point is thirty two above zero, it meant there were one hundred and seven degrees of frost. _____

Other Uses of the Hyphen

☆ *Use a hyphen if you must divide a word at the end of a line. (Divide words only between syllables. One-syllable words cannot be divided. When in doubt about dividing words properly, consult a dictionary.)*

       sing-ing   **black-board**

☆ *Put a hyphen after prefixes such as* all-, self-, pre-, *and* mid-.

all-aboard   **self-confidence**

☆ *Use a hyphen between the numerator and denominator in writing out fractions used as modifiers.*

      one-half full   **two-thirds majority**

☆ *Use a hyphen to serve for the phrase "up to and including" when used between numbers and dates.*

      pages 25-30   **May 15-20**

Try It!
Follow the instructions below for writing words and phrases that include hyphens.

1. Write the following words as they would be separated at the end of a line:
   working _____ surprise _____ instinct _____

2. Write a sentence using one of these words: self-conscious, mid-December.
   _____

3. If your organization needed to pass rules with 75% of the members agreeing, how would you write it? _____ majority (how many fourths?).

4. Write the numbers from 85 through 95 using a hyphen. _____

5. Write a hyphenated date that includes January 1 through 31. _____

Parentheses, Brackets, Dashes, and Hyphens in Action!

Try It!
The following passage from Edgar Allan Poe's "The Tell-Tale Heart" contains dashes, parentheses, and hyphens. Brackets containing explanatory information have been added to Poe's story. In the lines below, finish the story imitating Poe's writing style, using at least one each of parentheses, brackets, dashes, and hyphens.

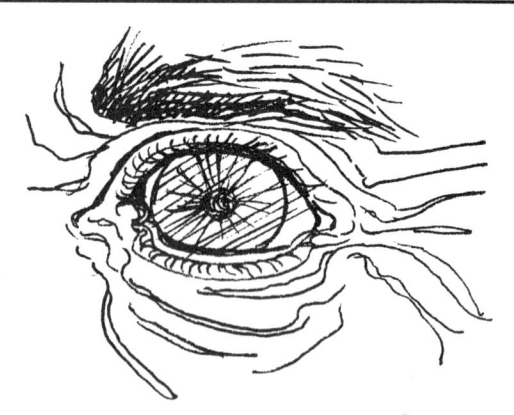

[The narrator begins the story asking the readers whether they think he is mad.] It is impossible to say how first the idea entered my brain, but, once conceived, it haunted me day and night. I loved the old man. He had never wronged me. I think it was his eye! Yes, it was this! One of his eyes resembled that of a vulture—a pale blue eye with a film over it. Whenever it fell upon me my blood ran cold, and so by degrees, very gradually, I made up my mind to take the life of the old man, and thus rid myself of the eye forever. You fancy me mad. But you should have seen me. You should have seen how wisely I proceeded—with what caution—with what foresight, with what dissimulation [deception], I went to work! I was never kinder to the old man than during the whole week before I killed him. And every night about midnight I turned the latch of his door and opened it oh, so gently! And then when my head was well in the room, I undid the lantern cautiously—oh, so cautiously—cautiously (for the hinges creaked), I undid it just so much that a single thin ray fell upon the vulture eye. His room was as black as pitch with the thick darkness (for the shutters were close fastened through fear of robbers), and so I knew that he could not see the opening of the door, and I kept pushing it on steadily, steadily. I had my head in, and was about to open the lantern, when my thumb slipped upon the tin fastening, and the old man sprang up in the bed, crying out, "Who's there?"

_____
_____
_____
_____
_____
_____

Italics
Titles, Names, and Words

☆ *Italics are a special typeface used in printing to indicate titles, names, and words used in a special way. Underlining may used to indicate italics.*

Use italics for titles of books, newspapers, plays, and magazines.
<u>The Adventures of Tom Sawyer</u>
<u>Chicago Tribune</u>
<u>Phantom of the Opera</u>
<u>Reader's Digest</u>

Use italics for names of ships, planes, spacecraft, and trains.
<u>Queen Elizabeth II</u>
<u>The Spirit of St. Louis</u>
<u>Friendship 7</u>
<u>Orient Express</u>

Use italics for foreign words and words used as words.
One way to greet a French friend is to say <u>bonjour</u>.
The word <u>green</u> has many different meanings.

Try It!
Complete these statements, underlining words that should be italicized.

The ship <u>Ecstasy</u> rescued people from the sinking cruise ship.

1. My favorite book is _____.
2. A magazine I often read is _____.
3. The name of the newspaper in my town is _____.
4. My favorite play is _____.
5. I can think of at least two meanings for the word _____.
   It means _____ and _____.
6. I know this foreign word: _____. It means _____.

Ellipsis Points Omissions

☆ *When quoting from a source, use three spaced periods to show that something has been omitted within a sentence.*

Original Passage: Aesop's fable, "The Boys and the Frogs"
Some boys playing near a pond saw a number of frogs in the water and began to throw stones at them. After killing several of them, one of the frogs lifted his head out of the water and cried out: "Stop, my boys: what is sport to you is death to us."

Quoted Passage:
This fable shows the insensitivity of using animals for sport. According to this fable, "Some boys playing near a pond . . . began to throw stones" at the frogs.

☆ *If the omission goes into another sentence, use four spaced dots.*

This fable shows the insensitivity of using animals for sport. According to this fable, after "Some boys playing near a pond saw a number of frogs in the water and began to throw stones . . . . one of the frogs lifted his head out of the water and cried out" to them to stop.

Try It!
Read the original passage above of "The Boys and the Frogs." Then, in the lines below, write the words that are omitted from the original.

1. "Some boys playing near a pond . . . began to throw stones" _____

2. "Some boys playing near a pond saw a number of frogs in the water and began to throw stones . . . . one of the frogs lifted his head out of the water and cried out" to stop them. _____

Slashes
Lines of Poetry

> ☆ *Use a slash to mark line divisions between two or three lines of quoted poetry that is run into a document. (More than three lines of poetry should be set off as an extended quotation.) Include a space before and after the slash.*

Original: From "The Cremation of Sam McGee" by Robert Service
"It's the cursed cold, and it's got right hold
    till I'm chilled clean through to the bone.
Yet 'tain't being dead—it's my awful dread
    of the icy grave that pains;
So I want you to swear that, foul or fair,
    you'll cremate my last remains."

Quotation run into the document:
Robert Service's poem "The Creation of Sam McGee" tells about the adventures and hardships of mining for gold in the bitter cold of the Yukon. McGee, a miner suffering greatly from the cold, asks the narrator to promise that he will be cremated if he dies there: "So I want you to swear that, foul or fair, / you'll cremate my last remains."

Try It
Borrow two or three lines from this later stanza of the poem, running them into the document that has been started for you. Use the slash properly.

    Some planks I tore from the cabin floor and I lit the boiler fire;
    Some coal I found that was lying around and I heaped the fuel higher:
    The flames just soared, and the furnace roared—such a blaze you seldom see:
    And I burrowed a hole in the glowing coal, and I stuffed in Sam McGee.

Toward the end of the poem, the narrator tells how he lived up to his promise to cremate Sam McGee: _____

_____

_____

© Instructional Fair, Inc.   IF2723 Punctuation

Italics, Ellipsis Points, and Slashes in Action!

Read the following poems from Carl Sandburg's collection *Chicago Poems*. The poem "Fog" describes fog coming into Chicago as though it were a cat. "Window" describes Sandburg's experience riding a train at night.

Fog

The fog comes
on little cat feet.

It sits looking
over harbor and city
on silent haunches
and then moves on.

Window

Night from a railroad car window
Is a great, dark, soft thing
Broken across with slashes of light.

Try It!

In a short essay, tell of some experience that makes you agree (or disagree) with Sandburg's observations in one of these poems. In your essay,

- refer to the title of one of the poems and to the name of the book in which the poem is found. Underline the book title to show that it needs to be italicized.

- quote from one of the poems, omitting some portion of it and showing the omission by three or four ellipsis points, depending on whether the omission includes the end of a sentence (or includes a period).

- include slash marks to indicate the ends of lines in the poem.

_____
_____
_____
_____
_____
_____
_____

Answer Key

End Punctuation   page 1
Periods follow these words:
London.	sound.
plate.	*Ladies.*
it.	Lady."

Declarative and Imperative Sentences   page 2
1. D   6. D
2. D   7. D
3. D   8. I
4. I   9. D
5. I   10. D

Interrogative and Exclamatory Sentences   page 3
1. !   5. !, ?
2. !   6. ?
3. !   7. ?
4. ?   8. !

Other Uses of the Period   page 4
Answers will vary.

Commas: Listening to What You Say   page 5
Answers will vary.
1. no
2. woman, her
3. increase

Applying Comma Rules: Introductory Elements   page 6
1. eating,
2. up,

Commas After Introductory Words and Phrases   page 7
1. Yes,   4. Admittedly,
2. cane,   5. knowledge,
3. Well,

Commas After Introductory Clauses   page 8
1. practitioner,   4. death,
2. views,   5. correct,
3. driveway,

Commas in Review   page 9
1. hypothesis,   4. Yes,
2. Obviously,   5. wealth,
3. entered,   6. affair,

Commas in Compound Sentences   page 10
1. wet,   4. him,
2. None   5. silent,
3. person,

Commas Between Items in a Series   page 11
1. illness, science,   4. London, luggage,
2. house, gig,   5. alarmed, lantern,
3. disbelief, fear,

Commas with Interrupters: Appositives   page 12
1. Mortimer, deceased,   4. interest,
2. Stapleton, health,   5. you, science,
3. No comma necessary

Parenthetical Expressions   page 13
1. Baskerville, Baskervilles,   4. family, denied,
2. companions, them,   5. image, me,
3. One, said,

Direct Address and Quotations   page 14
1. tale, sons, since,   4. so,
2. tragedy, Holmes, Nature,"   5. Now, Holmes,
3. words," Holmes,

Review: Commas with Interrupters   page 15
1. you," Holmes,   6. you, Holmes,
2. you, Holmes,   7. Baskerville,
3. Baskervilles, tragedy,   8. advice, it,
4. Charles, known,   9. man, of,
5. affected, explained,   10. Oh, Mortimer,

Commas with Nonessential Elements   page 16
1. Baskerville,   4. examination,
2. father,   5. Charles,
3. Baskerville, election,

1. two
2. one

Commas in Coordinating Adjectives   page 17
1. well-polished,   4. long,
2. successful,   5. high, curious,
3. tall, keen,

Commas in Conventional Situations   page 18
November 27,
Dear Watson,
April 11,
March 30,
Devon,
Sincerely,

Commas in Review   page 19
1. facts, Holmes,   5. luminous, ghastly,
2. grounds,   6. face, out, ground,
3. him,   7. body, fresh,
4. occurred,   8. Mortimer, instant, answered, Mr. Holmes,

Commas in Review   page 20
September 16,
Sherlock,
Library,
Street,
Sincerely,

Review: Multiple Commas Rules   page 21
1. excitement, hard,
2. course, correct, Nature,
3. in, Holmes, world,
4. tomorrow, Mortimer, here,
5. recommend, sir, cab, spaniel, door,
6. appointment, Mortimer, baronet,
7. small, alert, age, thick, strong,
8. "Now," Baskerville, me, Holmes, this,
9. Really, Holmes, imagined, Mortimer,

Commas in Action!   page 22
Answers will vary.

Correcting Comma Use in Revision   page 23
Answers will vary.

Semicolons with Independent Clauses   page 24
1. her;   3. advice;
2. born;   4. much,

Semicolons with Main Clauses and Conjunctive Adverbs   page 25
Answers will vary.

Semicolons with Other Punctuation   page 26
1. words;
2. will;

Semicolons in Action!   page 27
1. ten
2. six

Using Semicolons in Original Writing   page 28
Answers will vary.

Colons with Series and Lists   page 29
Answers will vary.

Misuse of the Colon with Series and Lists   page 30
were Russian
of the
as attending

Colons with Formal Quotations and Explanations   page 31
Answers will vary.

Colons in Conventional Situations   page 32
1. dwellings:
2. it:
3. words:
4. 9:00

Colons in Action!   page 33
Answers will vary.

Apostrophes with Contractions   page 34
1. wi
2. a
3. ha

1. he is, i
2. let us, u

1. I've, ha
2. It's, i

Apostrophes with Possessives: Singular and Plural Nouns   page 35
1. women's cars
2. bicycle's tires
3. pencils' erasers
4. doctor's orders

Apostrophes with Possessives: Compound Words   page 36
1. brother-in-law's
2. Sara's and Sam's
3. Erin's
4. Someone's
5. else's

Apostrophes with Numbers, Letters, Words   page 37
1. B's
2. 5's and 8's
3. no's
4. 1800s or 1800's

1. its, army's
2. "What's
3. veterans'
4. they'll
5. "That's
6. "I've

Apostrophes in Action!   page 38
1. I'm
2. don't
3. mother's
4. I've
5. Lord's
6. soldier's
7. mother's

Quotation Marks: Direct and Indirect Quotations   page 39
1. "I'll . . . do," said Beth, "we'll . . . ourselves."
2. Correct
3. "I . . . gloves."
4. "Some . . . hemmed,"
5. "I'll . . . pencils,"

Quotations with Long Passages   page 40
Answers will vary.

Quotations with Dialogue   page 41
"Ought . . . that?"
"It's . . . drying,"
"What . . . feathers,"
"There . . . ringlets,"
"Oh . . . hair!"
"You . . . hot,"
"It . . . fashion,"
"L . . . alone,"

Quotations Within Quotations   page 42
'If . . . this,'
'If . . . that,'
'When . . . grateful.' "

Quotations with Unusual Expressions and Titles   page 43
Answers will vary.

Quotations with Other Punctuation   page 44
1. "The Pickwick Club."
2. "The Pickwick Club": "Samuel Pickwick"; "Augustus Snodgrass"; "Tracy Tupman"; "Nathaniel Winkle."
3. "The History of Squash," "A Lament for S.B. Pat Paw,"

Quotations with Other Punctuation   page 45
1. Correct
2. Correct
3. back!"
4. Correct
5. you?" asked Jo.

Quotation Marks in Review   page 46
1. "Why. . . .happy,"
2. "I've. . .things,"
3. "We. . . .world," "Try . . . much"
4. "I. . .can," "But . . . manuscripts."
5. Correct
6. "I. . . .so?"
7. "There. . . .it,"
8. "If. . .Beth,"
9. Correct
10. "humble wanderers."

Quotation Marks in Action!   page 47
Answers will vary.

Parentheses: Explanatory Materials   page 48
1. (when. . .this).
2. (which. . .true).
3. (she. . .say).
4. (she. . .English).

Brackets   page 49
1. [she. . .listen]—
2. [obviously. . .lessons]."

Dashes with Explanation and Emphasis   page 50
1. cabin—that
2. 'cat-hole'—a
3. paper—the

Dashes with Appositives and Comma Series   page 51
1. destination—a
2. man—the
1. it—all
2. 'round"—that
3. women—some
4. begun—that

Hyphens with Compound Words and Numbers   page 52
1. freeze-up
2. spruce-covered island
3. thirty-two

Other Uses of the Hyphen   page 53
1. work-ing, sur-prise, in-stinct
2. Answers will vary.
3. three-fourths
4. 85-95
5. January 1-31

Parentheses, Brackets, Dashes, and Hyphens in Action!   page 54
Answers will vary.

Italics: Titles, Names, and Words   page 55
Answers will vary.

Ellipsis Points: Omissions   page 56
1. saw a number of frogs in the water and
2. at them. After killing several of them,

Slashes: Lines of Poetry   page 57
Answers will vary.

Italics, Ellipsis Points, and Slashes in Action!   page 58
Answers will vary.

© Instructional Fair, Inc.